Alice Beile-Bowes

Robin Hood and the Magic Trick

Ernst Klett Schulbuchverlag
Stuttgart Düsseldorf Berlin Leipzig

Zu dieser Lektüre gibt es eine Compact-Cassette,
Klettnummer 571331

Gedruckt auf Recyclingpapier,
hergestellt aus 100% Altpapier.

1. Auflage 1 13 12 11 | 2001 00 99

Dieses Werk folgt im Deutschen der reformierten Rechtschreibung und Zeichensetzung.

Alle Drucke dieser Auflage können im Unterricht nebeneinander benutzt werden, sie sind untereinander unverändert. Die letzte Zahl bezeichnet das Jahr dieses Druckes.

Zeichnungen: Walter Rieck, Heilbronn
Umschlagentwurf: Gebhardt, Korntal
Satz: Setzerei Lihs, Ludwigsburg
Druck: Manfred Dörler, Aichwald. Printed in Germany
ISBN 3-12-571330-7

Contents

Introduction

Robin Hood was an outlaw. The old stories tell us that he lived with his men and their families in Sherwood Forest, outside the town of Nottingham in England. We don't know when he lived, we don't even know if there really was a Robin Hood, but everybody in England knows stories about him.

Two of his best men were Little John and Will Scarlet. Maid Marian* lived with them, too. Her father wanted her to marry*, but she loved only Robin, so she ran away from home to live in the forest with the outlaws.

The Sheriff of Nottingham was Robin's enemy. He wanted to catch Robin, and he often sent his soldiers* to look for him. The stories tell us that many people hated the Sheriff because he was cruel, and because he took too much money from the poor people. But stories also tell us that Robin was the friend of the poor, and he robbed* the rich to help the poor*.

Sherwood Forest was much bigger then than it is today. There were only a few roads through it, and they were dark and narrow*. Robin's men watched every road, so that Robin always knew who went through the forest – a group of soldiers, a rich man with a bag of gold, a poor family, or perhaps a trader*.

introduction [ˌɪntrəˈdʌkʃn] Einleitung
Maid Marian [ˌmeɪd ˈmærɪən]
to marry [ˈmærɪ] heiraten
soldier [ˈsəʊldʒə] Soldat
to rob [rɒb] berauben
the rich, the poor die Reichen, die Armen
narrow [ˈnærəʊ] eng
trader [ˈtreɪdə] Händler

1. The horse trader

One day at Robin Hood's camp*, they heard that there was a horse trader on the road through the forest. He was on the way to Nottingham market with his horses.

"You know, Little John needs a stronger horse," said Will Scarlet to Robin. "He is far too heavy for our horses. They soon become tired when they are carrying him."

"You're right," said Robin. "Go and find this horse trader. If he is an honest* trader, and if he has a good strong horse — and if it doesn't cost too much, of course — buy the horse from him."

"And if he isn't an honest trader?" asked Will.

"Well, if he has a good strong horse but if he *isn't* an honest trader, perhaps the horse will just follow you off into the forest," said Robin.

Everybody laughed.

So Will Scarlet and Little John walked off into the forest to find the horse trader. When they reached* the road through the forest, they waited. Soon they could* hear horses' hooves*. They moved out into the road to meet the horse trader. But when the horse trader suddenly saw two men in the middle of the road, he was very frightened*. He didn't stop, but shouted to them, "Here, take this and leave me alone."

camp [kæmp] Lager
honest ['ɒnɪst] ehrlich
to reach [ri:tʃ] erreichen
could hier: konnte
hooves [hu:vz] Hufe
frightened ['fraɪtənd] verängstigt, erschrocken

Then he threw a little bag at their feet and rode away as fast as he could with his horses.

Will and Little John looked at each other and laughed.

"Well, well! He must have a bad conscience*!" said Little John. "And look, there are one hundred pounds in gold* in this bag! Robin will be pleased*!"

conscience ['kɒnʃəns] Gewissen
gold [gəʊld] Gold(stücke)
pleased [pli:zd] erfreut

"I think I recognized* that man," said Will Scarlet. "He isn't an honest trader. Do you know what he does?"

"No, I don't. Tell me."

"Well, his own* horse is a very good horse. And it is very clever, too. A lot of people want to buy it. But the horse trader always asks for too much money, of course, because he doesn't really want to sell it. But sometimes he meets a man from another part* of the country. He doesn't ask much for the horse. The man is very pleased, and buys the horse. After that they have a drink together. The horse trader pays, of course. He wants to find out where the man is going to and which road he is going to take. Then the horse trader hides in the forest near the road. When the new owner* of the horse rides past, the horse trader whistles*. Then his horse throws off its new owner, he falls to the ground*, and the horse runs into the forest back to the horse trader. But the new owner doesn't know that. He just thinks that he has lost his new horse."

"Well, the horse trader isn't a very honest man at all," said Little John. "Come on, let's go back to the camp and give the money to Robin."

"What do you think he will do with it this time?" said Will.

"I don't know," said Little John. "But he always uses it well." So they turned and began to walk back to the camp.

to recognize ['rekəgnaɪz] erkennen
own [əʊn] eigen(es)
part [pɑ:t] Teil
owner ['əʊnə] Besitzer
to whistle ['wɪsl] pfeifen
ground [graʊnd] Boden

2. Will and Little John meet the pot-and-pan man

On their way through the forest to the camp, Little John and Will suddenly heard a strange* noise. It came from behind a group of trees. They knew the noise somehow*. It sounded like* some small animal, but it wasn't an animal. What could it be? Then Will recognized the noise. He turned to Little John and smiled.

"It's a baby!" he said. "It's crying!"

But it didn't sound like a strong, healthy* baby. It sounded ill. Little John and Will came out of the trees. They saw a man with his wife and child and their cart*. On the cart were lots of pots* and pans*. It was a pot-and-pan man* with his family on his way to market. But something was wrong. The man's face was white and he held his head in both hands. The woman had the baby in her arms.

The pot-and-pan man and his family were frightened when they saw Will and Little John. The woman shouted, "Are you Robin Hood's men? Don't hurt* us! We are only poor people. We have no money."

"You needn't be afraid, we won't hurt you," said Little John.

strange [streɪndʒ] merkwürdig
somehow ['sʌmhaʊ] irgendwie
it sounded like [saʊndɪd] es klang wie
healthy ['helθɪ] gesund
cart [kɑ:t] Karren
pot [pɒt] (Koch-)Topf
pan [pæn] Pfanne
pot-and-pan man Kesselflicker und Händler für Töpfe und Pfannen
to hurt [hɜ:t] weh tun

"And we don't take money from the poor," added Will. "But tell us, why have you stopped here in the middle of the forest?"

"I don't know what to do," said the woman. "We have to go to the market with our pots and pans because we need the money. We had to pay the Sheriff's new tax* on carts, and that took all our money. We have nothing. And now my husband and our baby are ill. And I can't push the cart alone."

Little John turned to Will. "A tax on carts? I've never heard of that before! The Sheriff can't do that!" he said.

"They can tell us about that later," said Will. He turned back to the woman. "You must come with us to our camp," said Will. "We have a fire and warm food there. You can stay until your husband and baby are better."

"And when your husband is better," said Little John, "he can mend* some of our pots, or even sell us some new pots and pans."

The pot-and-pan man and his family were very glad. "Thank you for your help, thank you," said the woman. "My name is Anna, and my husband is called* Peter."

"My friend is called John Little," said Will, "but we call him Little John — because he is so big."

And Little John put his hand on Will's arm. "And this is Will Scarlet — we call him that because his clothes are red. He has another name, but we have all forgotten it!"

Then Little John lifted* the pot-and-pan man onto the cart, and he pushed the cart to the camp, while Will and Anna with her baby followed.

tax [tæks] Steuer
to mend [mend] flicken, reparieren
is called [kɔ:ld] heißt
to lift [lɪft] heben

3. At Robin Hood's camp

When they reached the camp, Little John explained to the others about the sick pot-and-pan man and his family. Everyone made the family welcome, and soon they felt better. Little John gave the horse trader's bag of gold to Robin. Robin was very pleased.

"I'm sure we can use this well," he said. Then he asked Anna some more questions about the Sheriff's new tax on carts. He was sure that this tax must be the Sheriff's idea, and that the money was for him alone.

Later that evening, when it was dark, they all sat round the fire. The pots and pans on the cart shone in the light of the fire.

Maid Marian said, "Look at the light on the pans! They look like gold!"

"You're right! If only we could turn* them into gold," answered Robin. "Eh, Marian?"

But there was no answer from Marian.

"Marian, are you dreaming?" said Robin.

"Mm? Oh! Oh, sorry, I've just had an idea ..." answered Marian.

"Well then, tell us about your idea."

"Well, I think I know how we could turn the pots and pans into gold." She whispered for a long time in Robin's ear. Robin was quiet for a time. "Well, what do you think?" said Marian.

"Well, it might work*," said Robin.

"Of course it'll work! You know how greedy* he is!" said Marian.

to turn hier: verwandeln
it might work es könnte klappen
greedy gierig

"He? Who?" said the pot-and-pan man.

"You'll see," said Robin. "Now, here's a bag of gold. It's from a horse trader with a bad conscience. I think I have found a very good use* for it. Will you sell me all your new pots and pans?"

"All my pots and pans? But you don't need so many!" The pot-and-pan man was surprised.

"Yes, I do," said Robin. "And will you lend* me your cart, too?"

"Well, yes, of course," said the pot-and-pan man. "But why do you need my cart?" he asked.

"I'm going to go to market tomorrow," said Robin.

"But people will recognize you," said Anna, the pot-and-pan man's wife.

"Not if I'm wearing your husband's clothes," said Robin, and laughed.

"And will you lend me your clothes, too, Anna?" asked Maid Marian. "Then I can go to market, too."

"Anything, you can have anything. Anything you want. You have helped us so much!" answered Anna.

use [ju:s] Verwendung
to lend [lend] leihen

4. Robin Hood and Maid Marian go to market

So the next morning, Robin Hood and Maid Marian put on Peter and Anna's clothes and pushed the cart with the pots and pans to market.

When they arrived at the market they untied the pots and pans. Then they began to put them out so that* people could see them. There were many people at the market. They looked at Robin and Marian with interest*.

"Look, there's a new pot-and-pan man today."

"Yes, I've never seen him before."

"I wonder where Peter and Anna are today."

"I really need a new pan, but I haven't got enough money."

"Perhaps the pot-and-pan man can mend your old pan again."

When Robin was ready, he began to shout.

"New pans for old, new pans for old."

"Bring us your old pans, and get new pans back," called Maid Marian.

"Why use your old black pot when you can have a lovely new shiny* one for nothing?" shouted Robin.

"Special offer*! Only today! Don't wait too long! There aren't many left*!" called Maid Marian.

The people looked at each other. They were astonished*.

so that damit
interest ['ɪntərest] Interesse
shiny ['ʃaɪnɪ] glänzend
special offer ['speʃl'ɒfə] Sonderangebot
left [left] noch da
astonished [ə'stɒnɪʃt] erstaunt

"New pans for old? It can't be true", said one woman.

"They must be crazy," said another.

"Crazy or not, I'm going home to get my old pans."

"So am I*," said her friend.

Soon the women came back with their old pans and exchanged* them. Now there were lots of people round Robin and Marian's cart. But nobody recognized them because they had Peter and Anna's clothes on.

so am I ich auch
to exchange [ɪks'tʃeɪndʒ] umtauschen

5. The Sheriff's servant

One of the Sheriff's servants* was at the market. He couldn't believe his ears when he heard "New pans for old." He ran back to the castle kitchens and began to put the pans into a basket. The Sheriff's wife saw him.

"Hey, what are you doing with those pans? Where are you going?"

"I'm going to get new pans."

"New pans? But that's too expensive."

"There's a pot-and-pan man at the market. He's exchanging new pans for old."

"New pans for old? That's crazy."

"Well, it may be crazy, but it's true. It's too good to miss*!"

"Yes, yes, you're right. Look, take these pans, too."

And the Sheriff's wife began to look for more pans.

Just then the Sheriff came into the kitchen. His wife explained about the pans. The Sheriff thought for a moment.

"There must be a trick," he said. "Nobody gives away something for nothing."

"You're right, my dear," said his wife. "Nobody throws away money like that."

The Sheriff turned* to the servant. "When you exchange these pans," he said, "talk to this pot-and-pan man a bit. See if you can find out what his trick is."

servant ['sɜ:vənt] Diener
it's too good to miss so etwas darf man nicht verpassen
to turn hier: sich wenden

"I'll try to find out his secret*," promised* the servant.

"If you can do it, I'll pay you well," said the Sheriff.

The servant and the Sheriff's wife collected all the old pots and pans in the castle. There were so many that they needed two baskets. So the first servant went with another servant, and he carried the second heavy basket.

secret ['si:krət] Geheimnis

to promise ['prɒmɪs] versprechen

6. The servant talks to Robin Hood at the market

When the two servants arrived at the market, many of the pots and pans were already gone.

The first servant asked the pot-and-pan man — Robin, of course — “We aren’t too late, are we?”

“No, no. I’ve still got some pans left,” said Robin.

“Are these pans too old?” said the second servant to Maid Marian. He showed her some pans with big holes.

“No, no, the older the better*,” she answered.

When the second servant and Marian began to exchange the old pans for new pans, the first servant took Robin’s arm and started to talk to him.

“Nice pans, these,” said the servant.

“Yes, the best in Nottingham,” said Robin.

“Expensive?”

“Oh yes. Top quality*. You’ll find none* better.”

“Tell me, what’s the trick?”

“No trick.”

“Must be.”

“No, there isn’t.”

“But you can’t give away expensive pans for nothing.”

“I don’t.”

“Don’t what?”

“Give them away for nothing.”

the ... *the* ... je ... desto ...

top quality ['tɒp'kwɒlɪtɪ] Spitzenqualität

none [nʌn] keine

The servant shook* his head. “I don’t understand,” he said. Robin walked up and down*. He pretended* to think for a minute. Then he turned to the servant.

“Can you keep a secret?” he asked the servant.

“Of course. A secret is always safe* with me,” answered the servant.

“Well, just between you and me …” began Robin.

“Yes?” said the servant.

Robin shook his head again and turned away.

“No, no. I’d better not* tell you,” he said.

“Oh come on. I won’t tell anyone.”

“Well — you see, I can turn old pots and pans into gold.”

“You can what? I don’t believe you.”

“Well, if you don’t believe me, forget it!”

“No, no. It’s just that it seems* impossible!”

“Then why do you think I give away new pans for nothing? Do you think I’m an idiot*?”

“Oh no, of course not.”

“But remember! It’s a secret.”

“Don’t worry. I won’t tell anyone. But how do you do it? You must tell me.”

“Ah well, I can’t tell you that, can I?”

And Robin turned back to the cart and began to look at the old pots and pans.

to shake [ʃeɪk] *shook* [ʃʊk] *shaken* [ˈʃeɪkən] schütteln
to walk up and down hin- und hergehen
to pretend [prɪˈtend] vorgeben, so tun als ob
safe [seɪf] sicher
I’d better not ich sollte lieber/besser nicht
to seem [si:m] scheinen
idiot [ˈɪdɪət] Dummkopf

Maid Marian and the second servant were ready. The cart was now full of old pots and pans, and the servant's baskets were full of lovely new pots and pans. The first servant thought. He couldn't go back to the castle without* the secret. But he didn't have the secret. So this strange pot-and-pan man must come to the castle. He sent the other servant home with the two heavy baskets, and turned to the pot-and-pan man.

"By the way*," he said, "the Sheriff would like to meet you. He has invited you to the castle to eat with him."

"To eat with him?" said Robin. "I'm sorry, but I am very busy today. I have to collect new pots and pans. I haven't any left."

"Well, this evening then?" said the servant.

Robin pretended again to think. "I'll tell you what, the Sheriff can come to meet me in Sherwood Forest tonight."

"Sherwood Forest?"

"Yes, and alone."

"But it will be dark. And what about Robin Hood?"

"Don't worry about him. He never hurts me or my friends."

So the servant left, and went to tell the Sheriff.

without [wɪˈðaʊt] ohne
by the way übrigens

7. The Sheriff and the pot-and-pan man in the forest

When the Sheriff heard about the gold, he was very excited, and he decided* to go and meet this pot-and-pan man in the forest. But his wife didn't like it.

"Alone," she said, "and in the dark*? It's too dangerous!"

"Don't worry, my dear. Think how rich we'll be!" answered the Sheriff. The Sheriff was more greedy than sensible*!

As it grew* dark, he rode out of the castle towards Sherwood Forest, with just one servant. When he reached the edge* of the forest, he saw a figure. It was Maid Marian, still in Anna's clothes.

"I am the pot-and-pan man's wife," she said to the Sheriff. "Leave your horse with your servant and follow me. I will take you to my husband."

The Sheriff got off his horse, left it with his servant and followed her. After a time they came to a clearing*. The sheriff saw someone near a big fire. It was Robin Hood, of course. But the Sheriff didn't recognize him in the pot-and-pan man's clothes. The cart with all the old pots and pans was there, too, under a tree.

"Welcome, Sheriff. You wanted to see me?" said Robin.

"Yes, I believe you can turn old pots and pans into gold?"

"Who told you that?"

"My servant. He spoke to you this afternoon."

to decide [dɪ'saɪd] beschließen
in the dark [dɑ:k] im Dunkeln
sensible ['sensəbl] vernünftig
grew [gru:] hier: wurde
edge [edʒ] Rand
clearing ['klɪərɪŋ] Lichtung

"And what if I can?"

"I'll give you one hundred pounds for the secret."

"One hundred pounds? Let me see your money."

The Sheriff took out a bag of money and took out one hundred pounds. Robin could see that there was a lot more money in the bag. He walked up and down and pretended to think. The Sheriff became worried. Perhaps one hundred pounds wasn't enough.

"Two hundred pounds. I'll give you two hundred pounds," the Sheriff said.

Robin pretended to be unsure*.

"Well, I don't know," he said. "Nobody else knows the secret."

"Don't take it!" said Maid Marian. "Perhaps the Sheriff will tell everybody; then we won't be able* to find any old pots and pans."

"Three hundred pounds," said the greedy Sheriff.

"All right," said Robin. "Give me the money, and I'll show you what to do."

unsure [ʌn'ʃɔ:] unsicher

we won't be able ['eɪbl] wir werden nicht können

8. The Sheriff's problem

"Now," said Robin, "give me your old pots and pans." The Sheriff was surprised.

"My old pots and pans?" he said. "But I haven't got any old pots and pans. My servant exchanged them all this morning for new pots and pans."

"Well, I'm sorry," said Robin, "but if you haven't got any old pots and pans, then you can't do the trick. You have come for nothing, I'm afraid."

The Sheriff was really worried now. What could he do? He looked round, and saw the woman under the trees beside the cart with the pots and pans.

"Lend me some of your old pots and pans," he said to her.

"No, there's no point*," she answered. "You can only do the trick if the pots and pans really belong to you."

The Sheriff thought. He had no old pots and pans. There were hardly* any old pots and pans in all Nottingham any more — they all belonged to this strange pot-and-pan man. Then the Sheriff looked at the cart again. The old pots and pans on the cart shone gold in the light of the fire. The Sheriff had an idea ...

"Let me buy your pots and pans. Then they will belong to me. You can get more old pans in the next town, but in Nottingham there are no old pans left."

"Well, you'll have to pay me well," said Robin.

"Yes, of course. Another two hundred pounds. Here you are. That's all I have."

there's no point [pɔɪnt] es hat keinen Zweck
hardly ['hɑ:dlɪ] kaum

"All right," said Robin. "You can have the old pots and pans."

The Sheriff was very happy. He was very close* to the secret now.

"I'll be rich," he thought, "richer than any man on earth. I'll send my servants all over the land to collect old pots and pans. Nobody will know why I want them," and he rubbed* his hands together.

He turned to the pot-and-pan man.

"Now tell me what I must do!" he said.

close [kləʊs] nahe
to rub [rʌb] reiben

9. Robin Hood's "magic trick"

"Well," said Robin, "this is what you must do. First you must make a circle with the old pots and pans."

So the Sheriff took the pots and pans one by one and made a large* circle.

"What next?" he asked.

"Now," said Robin, "you must take the largest pot, and put it over your head."

"Is that all?" asked the Sheriff.

"No," said Robin, "in one hand you must hold a pot and in the other you must hold a pan."

The Sheriff picked up a pot and a pan and held them out.

"Like this?" he said.

"Yes, that's right," said Robin. "Now, in a minute you must stand in the middle of the circle, shut your eyes, say the magic words* and turn around three times*."

"What are the magic words?" asked the Sheriff.

"Listen to them, and try to remember them.

Trees at my front and at my back,
Turn to gold this pan so black.
Sun in the sky, so high, so hot …"

"But the sun isn't shining. It's dark," said the Sheriff.

large [lɑ:dʒ] groß
magic words Zauberspruch
three times dreimal

"That doesn't matter*," said Robin Hood. "Be quiet and don't interrupt* me again.

Sun in the sky, so high, so hot,
Turn to gold this old black pot.
Birds of Sherwood Forest old …"

"Old birds?" said the Sheriff, surprised.

"No," said Robin, "old Sherwood Forest. Now will you please not interrupt me this time.

Birds of Sherwood Forest old,
Turn these pots and pans to gold."

Robin was quiet. After a time, the Sheriff said, "Is that all?"

"Of course that's all," said Robin in an angry voice. "Isn't that enough?"

"Oh yes, oh yes," answered the Sheriff. "Please don't be angry."

"Now listen again," said Robin. "I'm going to say the magic words once more, but only once!

Trees at my front and at my back
Turn to gold this pan so black.
Sun in the sky, so high, so hot,
Turn to gold this old black pot.
Birds of Sherwood Forest old,
Turn these pots and pans to gold."

The Sheriff practised the magic words until he was ready.

that doesn't matter das macht nichts
interrupt [ɪntəˈrʌpt] unterbrechen

10. The Sheriff and the trick

Then the Sheriff walked into the middle of the circle. He held a pot in one hand and a pan in the other, and on his head he had the largest, blackest pot. He shut his eyes. (He couldn't see anything anyway because he had the pot on his head.) Then he opened them again and said, "I've forgotten how the words begin."

"Trees at my front," said Robin.

"Oh yes, now I remember."

And the Sheriff shut his eyes, turned round three times and said the magic words as he turned.

"Trees at my front and at my back
Turn to gold this pan so black.
Sun in the sky, so high, so hot,
Turn to gold this old black pot.
Birds of Sherwood Forest old,
Turn these pots and pans to gold."

Then he stopped, dropped the pot and the pan from his hands, lifted the large black pot from his head and looked at the circle of pots and pans. They weren't gold, they were just as they were before. Black, old and full of holes. He turned to the pot-and-pan man.

"It's a trick! You say you can turn old pots and pans into gold. You lied*!"

"We can," said Robin.

"And we have done!" said Maid Marian. They threw off Peter and Anna's old clothes, and the Sheriff saw that it was Robin Hood

to lie [laɪ] lügen

and Maid Marian. The Sheriff was so surprised that he couldn't say a word. Robin Hood held up the bag of gold.

"You see this? I didn't lie. I have turned these old pots and pans into five hundred pounds in gold. You took that money from many, many poor people. You put a tax on carts and you wanted the money for yourself*. But I shall give it back to the poor people."

"That's my money. If you give it to the people, I'll take it back from them," shouted the Sheriff.

"Be careful, Sheriff," said Maid Marian. "If you try to take it from them again, we shall tell everyone this story. Goodbye!" And she and Robin turned and vanished* into the dark forest.

The Sheriff went back to the edge of the forest. His servant was still there with his horse. The servant was excited when he saw the Sheriff.

"Did you find out how he does it, sir? Did he tell you the trick?" he asked.

"Don't ever talk to me about pots and pans again," shouted the Sheriff. "And I don't want to hear about any more magic tricks. Do you understand!? Never again."

The servant didn't say anything. He was very surprised. He never found out why the Sheriff was so angry.

yourself [yɔ:'self] hier: dich selbst
to vanish ['vænɪʃ] verschwinden

Questions

Chapter 1

1. *Why did Little John need a stronger horse?*
2. *What did the horse trader do when Little John and Will Scarlet moved out into the road to meet him?*
3. *Why do you think the horse trader did this?*
4. *Why did the horse trader always ask too much money for his own horse?*
5. *Why did he have a drink with the new owner of his horse?*
6. *How did he get his horse back?*

Chapter 2

1. *How did Will and Little John find the pot-and-pan man and his family?*
2. *The pot-and-pan man and his family were frightened. But they didn't need to be frightened. Why not?*
3. *Why did the family have no money?*
4. *Why couldn't they go to market?*
5. *How did Little John and Will help?*
6. *How did Little John and Will Scarlet get their names?*

Chapter 3

1. *What did Robin Hood think about the new tax on carts?*
2. *Maid Marian had an idea. She said, "..."*
3. *Why did she have this idea?*
4. *What did Robin do with the bag of gold from the horse trader?*
5. *What else did Marian and Robin want from the pot-and-pan man?*

Chapter 4

1. *Why did the people at the market look at Robin and Marian with interest?*
2. *Robin and Marian did something strange. What did they do?*
3. *What did the people think about it?*
4. *Why did nobody recognize Robin and Marian?*

Chapter 5

1. *Who else was at the market?*
2. *What did he do?*
3. *What did he tell the Sheriff's wife? (He said, "...")*
4. *What did the Sheriff think? (He thought, "...")*
5. *What did he tell the servant? (He said, "...")*
6. *Why did another servant go with the first man back to the market?*

Chapter 6

1. *Why did the Sheriff's servant talk to the pot-and-pan man?*
2. *What was Robin's "secret"?*
3. *Why did the servant invite the pot-and-pan man to the castle?*
4. *Robin had a better idea. He said to the servant, "..."*

Chapter 7

1. *Why was the Sheriff's wife worried?*
2. *Why didn't the Sheriff recognize Robin?*
3. *Why did Robin pretend to be unsure?*

Chapter 8

1. *Why was the Sheriff worried?*
2. *Why didn't Robin lend his pots and pans to the Sheriff?*
3. *The Sheriff had an idea. What did he want to do?*
4. *What did the Sheriff want to do when he had the secret?*

Chapter 9

1. *What did the Sheriff have to do first?*
2. *What did he have to carry?*
3. *What did he have to do to make the magic work?*
4. *What did the Sheriff do when Robin said the magic words?*

Chapter 10

1. *What did the Sheriff hold in his hands, and what was there on his head?*
2. *Why did the Sheriff open his eyes again?*
3. *Why was the Sheriff surprised when he lifted the pot from his head?*
4. *When did the Sheriff know that the pot-and-pan man and his wife were really Robin Hood and Maid Marian?*
5. *Did Robin Hood lie? What do you think?*
6. *What will happen if the Sheriff tries to take the money from the poor people again?*